How to Generate High Quality Leads for a Sustainable Business Expansion

Your First 500 Quality Leads Guaranteed

Melody Chigozie N.

ISBN: 9798873164899

DEDICATION

This Book is dedicated to God Almighty

CONTENTS

CHAPTER ONE
Introduction to Lead Generation

Of course! Creating leads is an essential part of expanding a business and is essential to creating a productive sales pipeline. To put it simply, lead generation is the process of drawing in and obtaining leads or prospective clients who have shown interest in a business's goods or services.

Finding and interacting with people who show buying signals or fit the perfect consumer profile is the aim of lead generation. Through focused marketing and sales initiatives, these leads are then developed and turned into clients. Lead generation can be achieved through various channels and strategies. Digital marketing tactics, such as search engine optimization (SEO), content marketing, social media marketing, email marketing, and paid advertising, are commonly utilized to reach and engage potential leads online. Offline methods like networking events, trade shows, and direct mail can also be effective in generating leads.

The process typically involves the following stages:

1. Lead identification: This involves researching and identifying potential leads who are likely to be interested in the product or service being offered. This can be done by analyzing demographic data, online behavior, industry trends, and other relevant information.

2. Lead capture: Once potential leads are identified, their contact information is collected through various means such as landing pages, contact forms, gated content, or opt-in forms. This allows businesses to establish initial communication and further nurture the leads.

3. Lead qualification: Not every lead is ready to become a customer immediately. Lead qualification involves assessing the potential customers' level of interest, their needs, budget, and timeline. This helps businesses prioritize and focus their efforts on leads that are most likely to convert into customers.

4. Lead nurturing: After capturing and qualifying leads, it's essential to nurture them through personalized and relevant content, email campaigns, or other forms of communication. The purpose is to build trust and credibility, establish a relationship, and educate leads about the value and benefits of the product or service.

5. Lead conversion: When leads have been sufficiently nurtured and are ready to make a purchasing decision, the sales team takes over to close the deal. This involves addressing any remaining concerns, providing additional information, and guiding the lead through the buying process.

6. Lead tracking and analysis: It is crucial to monitor and track the performance of lead generation activities to understand the effectiveness of different strategies. Analyzing metrics such as conversion rates, cost per lead, and return on investment (ROI) helps optimize lead generation efforts and identify areas for improvement.

Effective lead generation requires a combination of strategic planning, quality content, targeted marketing campaigns, and a systematic approach to capturing and nurturing leads. By implementing successful lead generation strategies, businesses can fuel their sales pipeline, increase revenue, and grow their customer base.

CHAPTER TWO

Categories of Lead Generation

Seeds, Nets and Spears

Aaron Ross, author of the book "Predictable Revenue", uses a simple categorization of "Seeds, Nets and Spears" to describe his view of the main categories of lead generation.

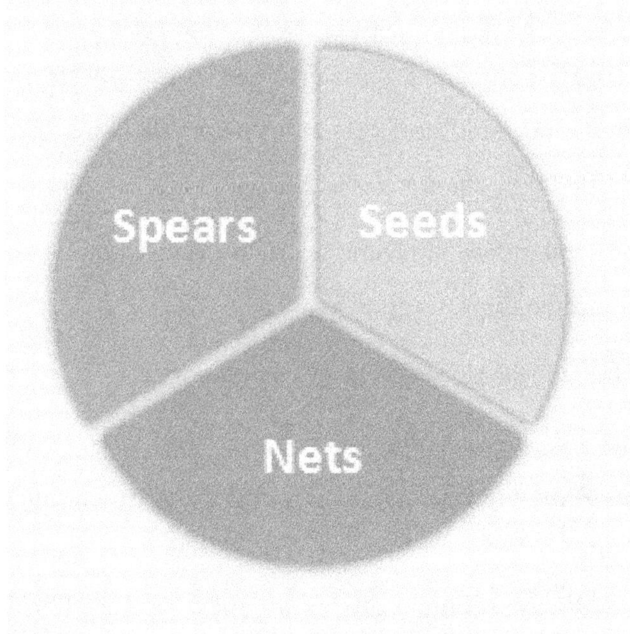

- ◆ "Seeds" are leads you generate through 'word of mouth'. For example, customer referrals or a lead passed to you by a partner.

- ◆ "Nets" are leads you acquire online through you website, blog and social media.

- ◆ "Spears" are leads you generate through outbound prospecting and lead generation

In 'Predictable Revenue' Aaron Ross suggests that business-to-business (B2B) companies should focus a lot of effort on this 3rd element – outbound lead generation using dedicated prospectors and a simplified process starting with email.

Our categorization is a little simpler than Brian Carroll's and a little more complicated than Aaron Ross.

There are 8 main categories of Lead Generation

- ✧ **Outbound** – prospecting and contact via email and phone
- ✧ **Online** – driving traffic to your website and generating enquiries and leads.
- ✧ **Paid 3rd Party** – content distribution networks, lead brokers, lead generation agencies, list vendors
- ✧ **Events** – tradeshows, invitational meeting, business breakfasts etc.
- ✧ **Branding & Advertising** – sponsorship and advertising in mainstream media, analysts etc.
- ✧ **Direct mail** – hard copy mailers sent to prospects

✧ **Referrals –** generating leads through customers and partners

✧ **PR –** press releases, editorials, speaking opportunities etc.

You can sub-divide these categories:

Category	Tactic
Outbound	<ul><li>Prospecting tools</li><li>Outbound email automation</li><li>Prospect databases</li><li>Phone prospecting</li><li>Lead Nurturing</li></ul>
Online	<ul><li>Content – strategy, creation, distribution</li><li>Website and Blog</li><li>Lead capture and marketing automation</li><li>Social media marketing</li><li>Email marketing</li><li>Webinars</li><li>Search Engine Optimization</li><li>Pay-per-click advertising</li><li>Display advertising and Re-targeting</li><li>Lead nurturing</li></ul>
Events	<ul><li>Tradeshows</li><li>Seminars</li><li>Executive briefings</li></ul>

Branding and Advertising	<ul><li>Advertising</li><li>Sponsorships</li></ul>
PR	<ul><li>Press releases</li><li>Editorials</li><li>ews coverage / interviews</li><li>Speaking opportunities</li></ul>
Referrals / Word of Mouth	<ul><li>Customers</li><li>Technology Partners</li><li>Service delivery partners</li><li>Professional networks</li></ul>
Direct mail	<ul><li>Promotional offers</li><li>Event invites</li><li>"Dimensional mail"</li></ul>
Paid 3rd Party	<ul><li>Lead brokers</li><li>Content distribution partners</li><li>List brokers</li><li>Lead generation agency / telemarkete</li></ul>

CHAPTER THREE
How to Choose Lead Generation Tactics

How do you choose which tactics to use? There are a few rules of thumb.

First, you should "fish where the fish are" – that means you should find out where your customers typically look for information and concentrate your lead generation there. For example, if they spend a lot of time on particular websites or are members of a professional association then you should look at tactics that can target those areas.

Secondly, assess the cost per lead for a particular tactic. For example, if you have a sale value over $5000 per unit then online pay-per click advertising may make financial sense i.e. you can afford to spend a few hundred dollars on advertising in order to acquire a customer. However, if you are a software vendor with an average sale price of $300 per year then online ads may not make financial sense and you will have to concentrate on low cost or free channels like social media.

Third, most lead generation tactics work better when they are used as part of a multi-channel approach. For example, leads will respond better when they hear about you across multiple touchpoints – through email, via web search, through their professional association and so on. Pick multiple tactics and synchronise them so that they reinforce each other. For example, combining email, PR and online ads in the periods before and after you exhibit at a tradeshow.

Fourth, consistent messaging is really important. Your promotional tactics should be reinforcing the same message across channels so that prospects are given a consistent description of what you offer and your competitive differentiators.

Finally, you should aim for a 'hub and spoke' model for your lead generation where most tactics are bringing prospects back to your website or phone.

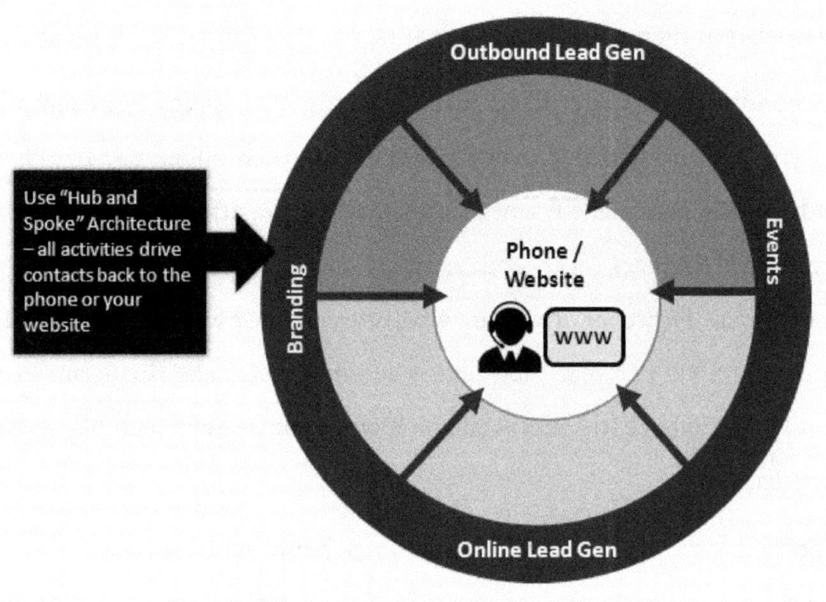

CHAPTER FOUR
Lead Generation Tips

Has your B2B business not had enough leads come through recently?

Maybe you're frustrated with the amount of money you're spending on inbound marketing, and you aren't seeing results as fast as you would like.

If this is the case, you aren't alone. Many companies spend a ton of money on different forms of marketing, only to find that qualified leads aren't coming in fast enough.

Outbound works, but if you aren't a fan of cold calling or aggressive marketing, you might be interested in trying out a LinkedIn lead generation service.

Not only won't your business come across as sleazy and aggressive, but if you choose the right Linkedin lead generation agency, you could be guaranteed 1 qualified lead per day (which amounts to 20+ leads per month.)

But the question arises…

How do you find this unicorn agency?

With so many different lead generation services out there, you need to choose one that will give you the best bang for your buck.

How do you do this? By asking these 10 questions

(Or if you're ready for a company that guarantees 20+ qualified leads per month, or your money back, set up a free 15-minute consultation call.

1. How long will it take before my first lead comes in?

Imagine paying an outreach agency, and signing a contract, only to have your first few leads come in a month later.

This would be disastrous. And unfortunately, this happens more often than not, with larger b2b lead generation agencies.

Have a look at some of these comments below from two different Linkedin Lead Generation agencies: (excluding the company names)

NOTE: We aren't adding these examples into this article to slam our competitors, but rather to focus on the fact that if you get locked into a contract, and don't have any leads after 4 months of paying, it's going to cause frustration. You don't want to find yourself in this situation.

No one wants to lose money.

So it's important to ask a company when your first quality leads will come in.

Because if you have the right target audience, and you have an ultra-targeted list of prospects, you should be getting your first qualified lead within the first 24 hours of launching your Linkedin lead gen campaign.

It's important to note though that the first week is usually the slowest when it comes to the lead generation process, but as you grow your prospecting sequence and follow up with prospects, then by week 8 the agency should have generated plenty of qualified leads for your business.

If an agency says that it takes time for leads to come in, it's important to ask them why.

Because if you have a defined target list, and you're selling to prospects who need what you're selling, then those leads should come in quickly.

IMPORTANT:

Your Linkedin profile can also play a major role in who accepts your connection requests or not. Remember the agency will have access to your profile to reach out to prospects as if they were you.

So if your profile is unprofessional, or has very little information on it, the chances of prospects wanting to engage with you will be minimum.

Here are some things to consider when updating your Linkedin profile:

Use your profile as a sales page. Many people use it as a resume, but this is an outdated way of using the platform. Your about section should tell readers exactly how your company can address their pain points and include any merits that your business has.

Below is an example of a great Linkedin profile:

- Notice how the contact details are clear at the end
- Pain points are addressed

- You know exactly what Dan Martell does.

- His photo is also clear and professional

2. How will you make sure that my Linkedin account won't get blocked?

If a lead generation company promises hundreds of leads, and that they send many messages per day, ask them how many messages will they send in a day.

Why? Because if the agency isn't careful you could be hit with these little beauties:

You don't want to be hit with these messages.

Not only does it slow down your outreach campaigns, but sending too many messages at once, will burn through your list.

At the same time, this is also important because the agency you choose should not only grow and nurture your connections, but they are connecting you with potential clients who will be part of your network even long after you stop working with the agency.

So if they are sending hundreds of messages that lack personalization, and you sound robotic in your messages, all it takes is one person to flag you.

This is really bad because then Linkedin will crack down on your account.

You need to make sure that your risk of getting blocked is under control.

If the agency is using crappy automation lead generation tools, like Dux-Soup, run for the hills. If they are using any browser automation tools, don't even go there.

The agency must keep messaging to a reasonable volume.

25 messages per day should be enough to hit your lead gen goals.

This amount can fluctuate, but never send more than 100 messages in one day.

Note: Interestingly enough, in the past 8 months, we haven't seen any restrictions at all on any level of volume on Linkedin for our clients. It's starting to look as if Linkedin is backing off on invite restrictions, as long as you're maintaining super high quality and reaching out to the right people.

3. How do you build a list of prospects?

If a lead generation service can't tell you how they build a prospect list, be wary.

When it comes to working with the best Linkedin lead generation agencies, they should be able to explain to you in detail how they intend to build a list of qualified prospects.

They should be able to tell you this on a sales call.

Don't feel as if you have to wait for them for weeks to have this process going.

A short conversation with a good list builder and a good agency should be able to tell you on a high level, exactly how they will find your prospects before working with you.

There's no secret to list building.

Here's an example:

Say now you would like to target agencies that offer video production services.

And you ask the lead generation company how would they target founders at these video agencies, they should be able to tell you the following:

We would start with clutch.co and search for video production/marketing agencies. Clutch is a directory of millions of agencies.

We scrape the relevant categories of agencies to get a broad list, there are going to be a lot of false positives there. We will then narrow it down according to data on your current buying customers.

For example, you would like to only target agencies that have at least 10 employees but not bigger than 200, because these are the types of agencies that are buying from you.

We would check this information through a program called Zoominfo for example, and then remove the agencies outside of the employee count range.

Next, we would scrape each website of these agencies to check whether they mention video marketing on their services page.

Then those who remain, we will use Linkedin Sales Navigator to find the founders or (decision-makers) of these agencies.

We will then check which founders are in your second-degree network, and then reach out to them via Linkedin messaging.

If a lead generation agency can't give you this amount of detail on the sales call, you might want to steer clear.

4. What type of leads will you get me?

This is an important question so that you and the agency are both on the same page. You might have one idea of a lead, and they might have a different idea.

There are also different types of leads.

Some leads mean getting your foot in the door to start conversations. Other leads might mean booked appointments.

You need to be very clear about what the agency means by "lead generation."

Double-check whether appointments will be booked for you, or if you will need to book the sales call with the prospect.

The agency should plan to start conversations in order for you to sell your product or service and aiding you get your fit in the door. Should also book appointments for you if you need the service.

It's also important to note though that the agency may not have an appointment setting service.

So if you are looking for someone who just fills your calendar and you don't have to respond to any leads, we are not for you.

But if you would like the following replies from leads:

Hi Harry, Sounds great, give me a call at your convenience,

Hi Sarah, Thanks for reaching out. Quick question: how much does it cost to make such an app? Thank

Can you send sample videos and the cost?

Hi Nick! Apologies for the delay here as I'm not on LI as much. Feel free to send a note to email so we can set up a time to chat.

5. Will I be locked into a contract?

Most lead generation services will lock you into a contract for a few months. And this is obviously not advisable.

WHY?

Because the results get customers to stay.

You should have clients who have been working with you for years without being locked into a contract.

There is a reason to stay on with the lead generation service for 3 months at least because, after this time, new leads really do ramp up.

But you should be happy within the first 2 weeks.

If there is a contract, ask the agency how long will you be locked into it for. 3 months? 6 months? A year? Find out exactly what it entails.

You don't want to be locked into a contract, and not see results. If the agency isn't generating leads within 2 weeks you should worry.

6. : Does the agency use personalization in their outreach and to what extent?

When it comes to a LinkedIn lead generation service, you need to make sure that they personalize their messages. And not just by adding a first name.

Why?

Because Linkedin outreach isn't going to be successful if messages are not ultra-personalized.

What does this mean?

Your Linkedin lead generation strategy should includes ultra personalization.

You should actually have personalization experts and all they do is research potential leads and write personalized messages just for the prospect.

How do you do this?

Google every prospect or check out their Linkedin profile. This should giveyou enough information to send them something personal.

Here is an example of how we write personalized messages in our outreach:

Hi {firstName}, {custom Intro}

After reading that you're working on {specific project responsibility} for {type_of_client}, I'd like to find out how you're dealing with {current pain point}. My company is working on new ways to handle {unique benefit} for {customer_type}, but I'm curious to hear what's been working for {Company} lately if you're open to exchanging ideas around {pain point}.

How's Thursday or Friday looking to connect?

Or

Alvin, loved your article on Mailshake about XYZ, particularly this point (XYZ) would love to connect with you.

When you think of personalization, think CCQ.

It stands for:

❖ Compliment

❖ Commonalities

Use the CCQ method for your copywriting. Find something to compliment the prospect on, a commonality, or ask them a question.

This captures their attention, and they reply.

Prospects are so used to being spammed on Linkedin, that they have blinkers on when new messages come through. If they receive the same generic automated message that gets sent out to everyone, they are going to ignore you.

An agency used the above method and this is a reply that they recently received from a prospect:

"Thanks for giving a sh*t about your leads! I don't respond to even 1% of LinkedIn messages but wanted you to know I appreciated you digging a bit. It makes a difference! Let's…"

A dentist and business owner wrote that after seeing our personalization.

Note: The personalization we included had something to do with how he enjoyed "water sports and camping".

Nothing fancy.

But there's no way you could deliver our "1 lead per day" if you didn't obsess about personalizing every single LinkedIn message.

So ask the agency that you decide to hire, do they use personalization, and to what extent.

If messages are not ultra-personalized, don't hire them. You're just going to be throwing money down the sink.

7. What expectations should I have for this partnership?

As mentioned above you don't want to be disappointed in the leads generated.

Perhaps in your mind, you're thinking that you want 500 leads in one month, but this isn't realistic.

Especially if you are using an agency that focuses on high-quality leads that will most likely convert once they get on a sales call.

This conversation is important.

IDEA: You might want to run some of your own LinkedIn campaigns before you hire a lead generation service. This can give you a realistic idea of what to expect. If you do decide to do this, ask yourself which messages worked? What didn't work? If you receive any data from your own campaigns, you could always share this with the agency, as this will give them a place to start.

 We can't say exactly what you should expect, because you might have an excellent product or service that's solving pain points, making prospects want to buy from you.

You might even already have a brand following through content marketing, social media, or SEO.

This means more people know about your product or service; which means they might be much more likely to book a sales call because your name is already out there.

Your product, your target market, and how new you are in the market will affect how many leads you can expect.

Running some campaigns yourself beforehand will give the lead gen agency a lot of firepowers to use.

Important: Be wary, though, if they don't ask you how you have been generating customers to date.

This is a fundamental question that shows the lead gen company what's working for you.

Even if you go to trade shows, use social media platforms, like Facebook, or use a specific pitch that works, let the lead gen agency know about it.

This will help them understand what's working for you and who they can target.

They can then add your copywriting/pitch to their Linkedin message copy, especially if it has been working.

Also, consider quality vs. quantity.

Be careful to tell the agency that you need X number of leads per week.

This might lead them to message way too many people, with no personalization, bringing the quality of your campaign down.

Focus on quality over quantity. Rather have 20 qualified leads who convert, than 200 random leads that aren't a good fit for your product or service.

Also keep asking for updates on what the Linkedin lead generation service is doing for you. It's okay and necessary to ask for stats, and what messages they are sending out.

Open and honest conversations about expectations are of utmost importance for success.

8. What should I provide in order to have more qualified leads coming my way?

Remember for a partnership to work, you also need to be able to provide data to the agency.

The agency that you choose has never worked with you before.

They don't know anything about your product or service and they don't know who your current buying customers are.

So give them tons of data.

If you have a list of companies who have purchased from you within the past 6 months, you need to share this information because it can help their sales teams to target the right people.

The more information you can share the better.

For example, perhaps many of your leads come from social networks like Twitter, then the agency knows that Linkedin might not be the best platform to find leads and that they should rather target prospects on Twitter. Remember not all prospects are on Linkedin.

9. How much will the lead generation service cost?

Costs vary from agency to agency, but most have similar pricing structures.

Some companies charge per lead; We don't advise this.

But according to research, you can expect to pay between $2000 – $5000 per month for a good Linkedin lead generation service.

B2B companies shouldn't be fooled though, into thinking that paying for cheaper services will get you the same results.

Some agencies don't charge too much, but the problem is that they might be neglecting an important marketing strategy like personalization and ultra-defined list building.

These cheaper agencies might even just buy a list of contacts and send hundreds of messages to everyone on the list.

This in our opinion is a waste of money and time. Rather pay a little bit more, and get better results that lead to higher conversion rates.

Important:

Know where you're at in your business.

What you can and can't afford, and most importantly, how much are these leads worth to you.

If you don't know your close rate from a lead to a new deal and where that deal ends up over the lifetime of the customer, then it will be hard to justify spending thousands of dollars a month on lead gen.

You have got to know the value of your customer and the value of each lead that comes in.

10. How do you find a good Linkedin lead generation service?

Lastly, this isn't a question for an agency, but rather a question to ask in general. With so many agencies out there, how do you find the right fit for your business?

Have a look at Linkedin, Google some Linkedin lead generation services, and have a look at their reviews. You could even ask friends or colleagues who they suggest.

But most importantly, ask to review case studies, hop on a consultation call, and ask the above questions. This will quickly help you pan out the good companies, from the not-so-great.

But if 20+ qualified leads per month sound good to you…

Get on a free 15-minute consultation call with the agency. There is no secret to generating leads. It starts with an ultra-targeted list of prospects, quality personalization, and real-time follow-ups (no bots).

CHAPTER FIVE
Understanding Your Ideal Customer Avatar

In the quest for perfect leads, clarity on your ideal customer is paramount. This chapter delves into the process of creating a detailed customer avatar, identifying demographics, psychographics, and pain points. By intimately understanding your audience, you lay the foundation for targeted lead generation strategies.

In the dynamic landscape of lead generation, a crucial first step is gaining a deep understanding of your ideal customer avatar. This involves creating a detailed and vivid representation of your perfect customer. Let's break down the key components of this process:

1. Demographics:

Start by gathering demographic information about your target audience. This includes age, gender, location, income level, and occupation. Understanding these fundamental aspects provides a foundational understanding of who your customers are in a broad sense.

2. Psychographics:

Move beyond demographics to delve into psychographics, exploring the psychological and behavioral traits of your audience. This includes their interests, hobbies, values, attitudes, and lifestyle choices. Understanding the motivations that drive your customers allows for a more personalized and resonant approach in your marketing efforts.

3. Pain Points:

Identifying the pain points of your ideal customer is a critical aspect of creating a customer avatar. What challenges do they face? What problems are they seeking solutions for? By empathizing with their struggles and challenges, you position your product or service as the solution they are actively seeking.

4. Creating the Avatar:

Combine the gathered information to create a fictional but highly detailed persona – your customer avatar. Give them a name, a face, and a backstory. The more specific and realistic this persona is, the better you can tailor your marketing strategies to resonate with real individuals who share similar characteristics.

5. Importance of Understanding:

Intimately understanding your audience goes beyond a mere exercise. It forms the bedrock of your entire lead generation strategy. When you know who your customers are on a personal level, you can craft targeted messages that speak directly to their needs and aspirations. This personalization significantly enhances the effectiveness of your marketing efforts.

6. Tailored Marketing Strategies:

Armed with a well-defined customer avatar, you can now tailor your marketing strategies with precision. Whether it's creating content, designing ads, or developing products/services, every decision can be aligned with the preferences and needs of your ideal customer. This targeted approach increases the likelihood of attracting and converting leads that resonate with your brand.

In essence, this chapter is a guide to constructing a detailed and insightful ideal customer avatar. It emphasizes that in the pursuit of perfect leads, clarity on who your customers are is not just beneficial but essential. The more intimately you understand your audience, the more effectively you can connect with them and guide them through the customer journey.

CHAPTER SIX

Crafting Irresistible Offers

Perfect leads are enticed by irresistible offers. Explore the art of creating value propositions that resonate with your audience. This chapter guides you through the psychology of crafting compelling offers that not only attract but also convert potential leads into loyal customers.

In the realm of lead generation, the ability to craft irresistible offers is a powerful tool. This chapter delves into the art and science behind creating value propositions that not only capture the attention of your audience but also convert them into devoted customers. Let's explore the key elements in detail:

1. Understanding Value Proposition:

Begin by understanding the concept of a value proposition. This is the unique value your product or service offers to solve a customer's problem or meet a need. It's the core message that communicates why your offering is superior to alternatives in the market.

2. Aligning with Customer Needs:

Crafting an irresistible offer starts with aligning your value proposition with the specific needs and desires of your target audience. Identify pain points or desires that resonate with them, and tailor your offer as a solution or enhancement to their current situation.

3. The Psychology of Perceived Value:

Explore the psychology behind how customers perceive value. It's not just about lowering prices; it's about increasing the perceived value of what you offer. This could involve bundling products or services, offering exclusive bonuses, or emphasizing unique features that set your offering apart.

4. Personalization and Relevance:

Irresistible offers are highly personalized and relevant to the individual needs of your leads. Leverage data and insights about your audience to customize your offers. This personal touch creates a connection and makes your proposition more compelling.

5. Building Urgency and Scarcity:

Understand the principles of urgency and scarcity. By creating a sense of limited availability or time-sensitive benefits, you instill a fear of missing out (FOMO) in your leads. This urgency can drive quicker decisions and conversions.

6. Clear Communication:

Crafting an irresistible offer requires clear and concise communication. Clearly articulate the benefits of your offer, making it easy for potential leads to understand how it solves their problem or fulfills their desires. Use language that resonates with your target audience.

7. A/B Testing and Iteration:

The chapter emphasizes the importance of testing different elements of your offer to understand what resonates best with your audience. A/B testing allows you to experiment with variations and refine your approach based on real-time data and feedback.

8. Post-Purchase Experience:

Crafting irresistible offers extends beyond the initial conversion.

Consider the post-purchase experience and how you can continue to deliver value. This could involve additional resources, customer support, or exclusive perks for loyal customers.

In summary, this chapter is a comprehensive guide to the art of crafting irresistible offers. By understanding the psychology of your audience, aligning with their needs, and creating a sense of urgency, you can develop offers that not only attract attention but also convert leads into long-term, loyal customers.

CHAPTER SEVEN

Leveraging Multi-Channel Lead Generation

Diversification is key in the pursuit of perfect leads. This chapter explores the landscape of multi-channel lead generation, from email campaigns and social media strategies to content marketing. Understanding the strengths of each channel and how they complement one another is crucial for a holistic and effective approach.

In the dynamic realm of lead generation, diversifying your approach across multiple channels is a strategic imperative. This chapter delves into the intricacies of multi-channel lead generation, elucidating the landscape from various perspectives. Here's a detailed exploration of the key components:

1. Recognizing the Importance of Diversification:

The chapter begins by emphasizing the significance of diversification in lead generation. Relying on a single channel poses risks, and a diversified approach hedges against uncertainties in any particular marketing avenue. This strategy is crucial for reaching a broader audience and maximizing your chances of connecting with potential leads.

2. Exploring Email Campaigns:

Delve into the world of email campaigns as a foundational element of multi-channel lead generation. Understand the nuances of crafting compelling email content, segmenting your audience for targeted communication, and utilizing automation for efficiency. Email remains a powerful tool for nurturing leads and guiding them through the sales funnel.

3. Social Media Strategies:

Explore the dynamic landscape of social media and its role in lead generation. Understand the strengths of each platform—whether it's the visual appeal of Instagram, the professional network of LinkedIn, or the engagement potential of Twitter. Crafting tailored strategies for each platform ensures that your message resonates effectively with diverse audiences.

4. Content Marketing Integration:

Content is king, and this chapter delves into how content marketing synergizes with lead generation. From blog posts and articles to videos and infographics, learn how to create valuable, shareable content that not only attracts leads but also positions your brand as an authority in your industry.

5. SEO Strategies:

Understand the crucial role of Search Engine Optimization (SEO) in multi-channel lead generation. Explore how optimizing your content for search engines enhances visibility and attracts organic traffic. A well-executed SEO strategy complements other channels by driving sustained, long-term traffic to your digital assets.

6. Paid Advertising Tactics:

Delve into the world of paid advertising, whether through Google Ads, social media ads, or other platforms. Understand how targeted paid campaigns can quickly amplify your reach and attract leads with specific interests. This section explores the importance of budget allocation, A/B testing, and tracking ROI for paid efforts.

7. Holistic Approach:

The chapter underscores the importance of a holistic approach where each channel complements the others. Rather than viewing channels in isolation, understanding how they interact and support one another ensures a cohesive and effective multi-channel strategy.

8. Analytics and Optimization:

The final section emphasizes the significance of analytics in measuring the performance of each channel. Utilize data to optimize your strategy continuously. Identify which channels are delivering the most valuable leads and adjust your approach accordingly for maximum impact.

In conclusion, this chapter is a comprehensive guide to navigating the multi-channel landscape in lead generation. From email campaigns and social media to content marketing and paid advertising, understanding the strengths of each channel and integrating them strategically forms the backbone of a holistic and effective lead generation strategy.

CHAPTER EIGHT

Implementing Data-Driven Lead Scoring

In the journey to acquire perfect leads, not all prospects hold the same potential. This chapter introduces the pivotal concept of data-driven lead scoring, a systematic approach to distinguishing and prioritizing leads based on their behavior and interactions. Here's a detailed exploration of the key components:

1. Understanding Lead Scoring:

Commence with a comprehensive understanding of lead scoring. This involves assigning numerical values to leads based on their activities, engagement, and attributes. The numerical score serves as a quantitative representation of a lead's likelihood to convert into a customer.

2. Behavioral and Demographic Factors:

Explore the myriad factors that contribute to lead scoring. Behavioral aspects, such as website visits, content downloads, and email interactions, are crucial. Additionally, demographic factors, including job title, company size, and industry, can be incorporated to create a holistic profile of each lead.

3. Establishing Scoring Criteria:

Define and establish clear criteria for lead scoring. Work

collaboratively with sales and marketing teams to identify key indicators of lead quality. Whether it's a certain number of page visits, engagement with specific content, or filling out a contact form, these criteria become the basis for assigning scores.

4. Automation and Integration:

Implement automation tools to streamline the lead scoring process. Integrate your Customer Relationship Management (CRM) system with marketing automation tools to ensure seamless data flow. This integration enables real-time scoring updates and ensures that your teams are working with the most current information.

5. Weighting Scores:

Understand the importance of weighting different activities or attributes in lead scoring. Some actions may be more indicative of a high-quality lead than others. Assign appropriate weights to different criteria based on their significance in the customer journey and buying process.

6. Collaboration between Sales and Marketing:

Foster collaboration between sales and marketing teams. Effective lead scoring requires alignment between these two departments. Regular communication ensures that the criteria remain relevant, and the scoring system evolves to meet the changing needs of both teams.

7. Continuous Optimization:

Emphasize the iterative nature of lead scoring. Regularly analyze the effectiveness of your scoring system and make adjustments based on performance data. Continuous optimization ensures that your lead scoring remains adaptive to market changes and evolving customer behaviors.

8. Feedback Loop and Analysis:

Establish a feedback loop for ongoing analysis. Encourage regular communication between sales and marketing to gather insights into lead quality and conversion rates. Use this feedback to refine scoring criteria and maintain a dynamic and responsive lead scoring system.

9. Resource Optimization:

The ultimate goal of lead scoring is resource optimization. By focusing efforts on leads with higher scores, your sales team can prioritize their time and energy on prospects more likely to convert. This not only increases efficiency but also maximizes the impact of your lead generation efforts.

In summary, this chapter provides a detailed guide on implementing a data-driven lead scoring system. By understanding the nuances of behavioral and demographic factors, establishing clear criteria, leveraging automation, and fostering collaboration, you can optimize your resources and ensure that your sales team is focusing on leads with the highest potential for conversion.

CHAPTER NINE

Nurturing Long-Term Relationships

In the pursuit of perfect leads, recognizing that they are more than one-time transactions is fundamental. This chapter delves into the significance of lead nurturing strategies, emphasizing the creation of sustained, long-term relationships. Here's a detailed exploration of the key components:

1. Concept of Long-Term Relationships:

Begin by understanding the intrinsic value of long-term relationships. Perfect leads are not merely customers; they form the bedrock of sustained business growth. Fostering relationships that extend beyond the initial transaction is key to building brand loyalty and advocacy.

2. Drip Campaigns:

Explore the effectiveness of drip campaigns as a lead nurturing strategy. Drip campaigns involve sending a series of targeted, automated messages to leads over time. This gradual and strategic approach keeps your brand consistently in the minds of your leads, providing valuable content and nudging them through the customer journey.

3. Personalized Content:

Understand the power of personalized content in nurturing long-term relationships. Tailoring your messaging and content to the specific needs and preferences of individual leads enhances engagement. This personalized approach demonstrates a genuine understanding of your customers and reinforces a connection with your brand.

4. Continuous Engagement:

Emphasize the importance of continuous engagement beyond the initial conversion. Regularly communicate with your leads through various channels—email newsletters, social media, webinars, etc. Consistent engagement keeps your brand relevant and positions you as a trusted resource.

5. Customer Education and Support:

Nurturing relationships involves more than promotional content. Provide valuable resources that educate and support your leads. This could include how-to guides, tutorials, or exclusive access to industry insights. By offering ongoing value, you strengthen your position as a partner in their success.

6. Loyalty Programs and Incentives:

Explore the implementation of loyalty programs and incentives. Recognize and reward customer loyalty with exclusive offers, discounts, or special access. These initiatives not only show appreciation but also encourage repeat business and positive word-of-mouth.

7. Leveraging Customer Feedback:

Actively seek and leverage customer feedback. Establish channels for communication where leads can share their experiences, preferences, and suggestions. This feedback loop not only helps in refining your offerings but also makes your leads feel heard and valued.

8. Referral Programs:

Recognize the potential of referrals in long-term relationship building. Implement referral programs that incentivize existing customers to refer others. Word-of-mouth marketing from satisfied customers is a powerful driver of organic growth.

9. Measuring and Adapting:

The chapter emphasizes the need for measuring the effectiveness of your lead nurturing strategies. Utilize analytics to understand engagement levels, conversion rates, and customer satisfaction. This data-driven approach allows for continuous adaptation and improvement.

10. Integration with Sales:

Lastly, highlight the importance of integration between lead nurturing efforts and the sales process. Seamless collaboration between marketing and sales ensures that leads nurtured effectively transition into long-term, loyal customers.

In summary, this chapter provides a comprehensive guide to nurturing long-term relationships with perfect leads. From drip campaigns and personalized content to continuous engagement and loyalty programs, the strategies outlined contribute to the creation of a customer-centric approach that goes beyond individual transactions, fostering sustained growth and success.

ABOUT THE AUTHOR

Melody Chigozie N. is a renowned expert in the field of digital marketing and lead generation. With over 5 years of experience in the industry, he has successfully helped numerous businesses boost their revenue through targeted lead generation strategies.

He has an extensive background in marketing and sales, which provides him with a unique perspective on lead generation. He has spent years working in various marketing roles, including overseeing digital marketing campaigns, managing lead generation teams, and optimizing sales funnels.

Through his extensive experience, he has developed a deep understanding of the intricacies of lead generation and the strategies required to generate high-quality leads. He possesses a comprehensive knowledge of various digital marketing channels, including email marketing, social media marketing, content marketing, and search engine optimization (SEO).

The author also has a remarkable proficiency in data analysis, leveraging analytics tools and metrics to identify trends, optimize campaigns, and maximize conversion rates. His data-driven approach ensures that the lead generation strategies outlined in the book are effective and results-oriented.